Come Walk

With Me

To God I Have Value; To God I Am Loved; To God I Am Forgiven.

Ellen Reece-Jarman

Come Walk with Me
ISBN 978-0-9823390-7-7

HOPE MINISTRIES
Ellen Reece-Jarman
8510 S. Clark Rd
Nashville, MI 49073
hopeministries017@gmail.com

KINGDOM
Ministry
Publications

4801 Willoughby Rd • Holt, MI 48842
☏517-648-6040   🖷517-709-3112
kmp@cfcholt.com

TABLE OF CONTENTS

FOREWORD

I have the privilege of knowing Elly Reece-Jarman, a great encourager and woman of God. We met in a church in Nashville, Michigan where my husband and I were preaching. During one particular service as I was speaking I felt the Lord was ministering to her about her future, telling her that He had more for her to do. After the service she came up to me and told me she felt the same thing in her heart. This book, and the books to follow are a result of that word from the Lord.

As I have been reading, my heart breaks and then rejoices again and again as I learn her life story. From infancy her life has been challenged at every turn but God brought her through. This book is a testimony of the power of God to save, heal and deliver in the face of unimaginable tragedy.

I know you will be blessed and your heart will be strengthened as you read. The Lord truly is in love with us, and will move on our behalf constantly to guard and keep us. Elly's life is a testament to His love and His overcoming power.

—Rev. Deborah Moore

COME WALK WITH ME

Chapter One
THROWN AWAY

Many people around the world celebrate bringing in the New Year. Parties get underway the evening of December thirty-first and are in full swing well before midnight.

It is a time when people forget the pain of the past year and look forward to the joy that this new year may bring them, an opportunity to make peace with their past and look forward to making the coming year a happier one having a clear conscience.

Sometimes gifts are given to that "special some-one" to show love and deepest devotion.

A time of new beginning towards the direction

of their choice, tears of happiness beyond words that only action of the heart can express. Tears of sadness for those not with us any more, yet the heart holds the treasured memories of time well spent and forever grateful for the days of laughter exchanged.

Three minutes past midnight on New Year's Day 1954 I was delivered into this world. My mother had been out with her father celebrating and on the short walk home her water broke. My grandpa helped my mother towards our small apartment and as she put her foot over the front door step into the family room, I arrived; a disappointment to mother from my first breath. Mother had been told over and over again by close friends and family members that she was carrying a boy, and believed what she heard with all her heart. But it was not meant to be.

> *Jeremiah 1:5 KJV*, *"Before I formed thee in the belly I knew thee; and before thou camest forth out of the womb I sanctified thee, and I ordained thee a prophet unto the nations."*

I was seven pounds of pure sweetness with a shock wave of very thick black hair, skin so white you would have thought I was made from milk. My grandma wrapped me in her shawl and there I lay in her arms safe and sound. Grandma had been taking care of my two-year-old sister for the evening when we came bursting through the door huffing and puffing. She knew the signs of labor having had five daughters of her own.

My father was not present at my birth due to his employment as a long distance truck driver so we did not meet until well into January. I can't say I remember his voice or his face but I do remember his smell. My grandma told of the times when he was home he would put me on his chest so that my little face could snuggle into his neck which in turn brought the biggest smile of contentment upon my father's face.

My grandma on my mother's side played a big part in caring for me in those early days since she lived in the house next to ours. As the year moved into spring my grandma got sick and was not able to help with my care any longer. Soon she was bedridden so my mother had to cope with two baby girls two and under mostly on her own. Summer and fall came and went with my grandma stabilized at home then the hard winter months hit. It was in November of 1954 at the age of eleven months that my tiny world was about to change.

At the bottom of the back garden separated by a three-foot wire fence is a small stream that ran through public land. Camped high on the hill to the north of our home were a group of travelers known as gypsies. Nana Deedor was their voivode or lifetime leader who looked after the welfare of the women and children. Nana Deedor 'saw' a child out in the open wearing only a diaper in the dead of winter. She 'heard' my cry for help and sent four of her trusted young men to find the baby. They found me just as Nana Deedor had seen. They placed me into her loving gentle arms. This wonderful woman was going to take care of me and raise me up as if I was her very own child.

Over the next four years Nana Deedor and I did everything together. She taught me the life of a gypsy. I learned that we were always on the move going from place to place as the land allowed. People did not welcome us with open arms. We had to make a living by the gifts and talents we each had. Often in the evening we would sit around the campfire and share stories of the men and women of old, telling of their hardships and triumphs. Among our gypsy family group were many musically talented folk and this was one of the ways we received most of our income. Before the people from the town came to watch us perform Nana Deedor would speak out our motto over us, "Rromano", "Rromano" which translated means to behave with dignity and respect. Our women were very beautiful with their jet-black hair and olive skin.

Their headbands were decorated with golden coins displaying prosperity and generosity towards others. They danced to tunes so well loved and so well known. I sat on Nana Deedor's crossed legs on the ground and watched enthralled as the orange and red fabric of their full skirts came alive with movement as they danced late into the night. Once the strangers were gone, Nana Deedor and I would sleep together, sometimes on the ground under the wagon smelling the hay and hearing the horses nearby or inside her brightly painted wagon on soft beds of hay. Happy days seemed to run into each other.

As my fourth birthday was fast approaching it was decided we would move back to where they had found me. Camp was set up on the top of the hill to the north of my birth home yet I had no idea this is where it all started. To earn income, Nana Deedor would make paper flowers and sell them in the main town square. She would often take me with her. I would sit at the top end of the pram surrounded by all the brightly colored flowers Nana Deedor had made. What a gifted lady she was!

Nana Deedor would sit on an old box next to my pram and sing away to the people listening. Sometimes they would buy her flowers and sometimes they would give her money just for singing. Once I got money for doing a little jig while she sang. Nana Deedor loved me beyond words and I loved her right back. Her toothless grin lit up her whole face. Her long very grey and orange hair was mostly covered with a headband. As we walked out of the square that day Nana Deedor saw a sign pinned to the wall that would change her life and mine forever. The sign read MISSING CHILD with details that moved Nana Deedor's heart to the greatest pain she would ever experience. Over the next few days Nana Deedor was quiet. Her mind was preoccupied with deep thoughts mingled with tears. She never left my side yet I knew she was troubled. I put my thin little arms around her neck and placed my face deep into the folds of her neck and held her with all my might as if to say, "It's gonna be ok. You'll see," but it wasn't going to be ok and she knew why.

That evening Nana Deedor let the rest of the family read the missing child poster she had taken down from the wall in town. I watched as one by one they read it, their faces sad as they looked our way. Each understood what should be done but no one said a word. This decision had to be made by one person. That person knew it. They all knew it. After a few days Nana Deedor made her decision and called us all together to share what her heart knew was the only answer. She would have the men go into town and find the man who had posted the missing child poster and bring him back to the camp.

The following days passed without entertainment, without singing, everyone locked in their own world working in silence. Nana Deedor kept watching and waiting for something to arrive but what? I was lost in watching the campfire dance displaying its bright colors of orange, blue and red when I heard a dog barking warning us of approaching strangers coming from across the field. The men had returned, with them a stranger. Who was he? Why was he here? What did he want of us? The stranger was made welcome and dinner was soon served. He sat across from Nana Deedor and me and every once in a while I would catch him looking at me. I felt safe. I was sitting with my Nana. Nothing and no one could get to me. She would never allow anyone to hurt me and live. Yet this man didn't seem like a man to want to hurt us. He spoke with a gentle voice. He smiled a gentle smile. Did he know me? Did I know him? Beginning to feel emotions I had never felt before I moved even closer to Nana Deedor. She gently took my hand and turned me to face her while still sitting on the ground. "Little one," she said, "I have something to tell you." Then in words I tried very hard to understand she lovingly told me the story of when I was found and my brief gypsy life. There was only silence when she finished. I turned to look at the stranger who hadn't taken his eyes off me. I felt afraid and brave at the same time because Nana Deedor's hand was on my back gently rubbing, soothing me. I moved slowly toward the stranger until I stood close enough to touch his face.

"Who are you?" I asked.

He replied, "I believe I am your daddy."

"How do you know that you are my daddy?" I asked him.

He smiled at me and said, "I have been looking for my daughter for a very long time. She went missing as a baby from my garden. I have searched these past years because I knew in my heart as her daddy that she was alive somewhere. Now I believe I have found her and she is standing right here in front of me."

I was not convinced! Then he asked if he could hug me. He opened his arms wide so I stepped in. Mighty yet gentle arms held me as I placed my face in his neck.

I took a deep breath and started to shake. I knew that smell.

"DADDY! DADDY! You found me!"

The next day my daddy and I prepared to leave

the only home I had ever known, the only family I had ever had, the only Nana Deedor I would ever love or be loved by.

It was a positive parting with hugs and smiles and happy chatter from my gypsy family.

Then I turned around and there was my Nana Deedor with arms open wide waiting just for me. The biggest smile graced that pretty weathered face, holding back the tears waiting to fall. Usually I hugged her when she was sitting down. Now she seemed so much taller. I guess she read my mind because she held me and lowered us to the ground. I was able once again to put my face into the folds of her neck and take her smell with me for the very last time. She reminded me of the things I had learned while in her care, to behave with dignity and respect.

Starting over in a home that does not move was not easy at first. No smells of horses, no smell of hay, no smell of Nana Deedor. I had a new family now and had to learn new rules of this family life. Grandma had moved and found a house next to hers that we lived in so once again we lived side by side. My father was gone a lot of the time with his work and Grandma helped where she could but I was given the responsibility of taking care of things and soon found myself doing just that while Mother slept. My older sister had no idea how to clean or cook so it was up to me to feed the family and keep the house clean. Mother was very pleased that I did it so well and told me that from now on it was my job. My baby brother was easy to care for. Mother had the milk all ready for him. All I had to do was feed him, burp him, and diaper him when she was sleeping. At ten months old my baby brother passed away and Mother blamed me. From that day on I was the target of her hate.

Christmas was fast approaching and Grandma had given me some paper to decorate and hang up. We had a real Christmas tree given to us by a family member. Tinsel made the tree look great. Dad was not able to come home for Christmas due to his work schedule. Mother had gift boxes wrapped in bright paper, all but one, that was wrapped in newspaper. Each gift had a number on it instead of a name. This was a game, or so I thought. Grandma and Grandpa came over for the Christmas meal and once I had cleared everything away it was time to open gifts. Mother gave out number cards to each one of us starting with Grandpa and Grandma. Grandpa got a new pair of socks. Grandma was next; she got a new handkerchief. Then my older sister ripped open her box to reveal the most beautiful doll that I had ever seen. She squealed in delight. Now it was my turn. I very carefully took the newspaper off my box and opened it. It was empty! Reading my thoughts Mother was quick to cover her hate of me by saying, "It's not empty, it's full of love." Could this be true? Had she realized her son's death was none of my doing?

I was the younger sister so clothes were passed down to me. I vividly remember the first time I had a new outfit. Mother went out to the stores and brought me a brand new outfit that made me look like a princess. The white lace dress fit like a glove. My new dress ended at the knee with a red trim all around the full skirt. I danced in a circle going faster and faster. The skirt flared out just like my gypsy sisters' skirts did when they danced and my heart took flight. I was lost in the happy memory for a moment until Mother's voice sounded loud and clear. The red jacket was also snug on me yet completed the outfit of sweetness and innocence. White lace socks and bright red new shoes made Mother smile in achievement. Mother fixed my hair and put red lipstick on my mouth. She stood back to see her work. Smiling to herself she led me to the window that looked out onto our front garden.

"Let me know when a big black car arrives." Then she disappeared into the kitchen.

I did look beautiful. I was wearing brand new

clothes but something was not right. I had to tell mother that she had forgotten something. I had to tell her that I needed underwear too. I waited by the window and sure enough a big black car pulled up. A very large man walked up our garden pathway all the while looking right at me. Mother answered the door and the two of them spoke briefly. The man handed her money and she smiled and said, "Thank you. So you like what you see?"

"Oh yes," said the man.

Mother reached down to remind me to "be a good girl." I was able to tell her that I didn't have any underwear on. She smiled at me and said, "You won't need underwear where you're going."

The stranger and I sat holding hands in the back seat of his car. A little while later we arrived at a very large house surrounded by trees. The big double iron gates opened as the driver rang the gate bell. The driveway was wide with flowers on both sides. Everything looked so pretty, so clean, so new to me. The bright red front door stood way back from the driveway and gave the impression of a large entrance. The driver got out and came around to my side of the car to open my door. He was wearing a very smart black uniform with a black cap to match. He lowered his head as we got out of the car so I lowered my head as if to say "Thank you for the ride."

I could hear music and people talking as we walked closer to the house. Children's voices filled my ears and I was thankful that I would have someone to play with. A lady with a black dress and a white apron on like my Grandma's opened the door and invited us in. We entered a very large room with sparkling lights that dripped down from the ceiling. A silver mirror hung in the middle waiting to be switched on. White linen tablecloths that hung to the floor covered the two food tables against the back walls. Most of the grown-ups were standing by a table being served big people's drinks, all the while talking and laughing. The lady who had answered the door led me to the room where the children were playing together. Over by the window a table stood laden down with all sorts of "kid's food" and pop. Most of the children had already eaten when I got there so I sat down on a small stool and waited with the other kids. Mother had told me not to get dirty or spill any food on my new clothes.

New Year's Day Party baby, that was I. Being sold into slavery to please others.

COME WALK WITH ME

Chapter Two
SAYING GOODBYE

These men and women were not family members, yet I had to call them "uncle and auntie." No names were used other than these. What gave them the right to hurt me and the other children the way they hurt us? Did our parents know what was going on behind closed doors? Were all these children sold just like I was and for the same sick reason?

I closed my mind off to my surroundings, to the cries I could hear from some of the other children. I closed my mind to the questions swimming around in my head, but most of all I closed myself to my pain, to my brokenness, to my innocence lost at the hands of a monster. I knew I never wanted to be here again or have anything to do with any uncle or auntie that came calling to my house asking if I could go and play with them. I had to find a way to escape this nightmare of shame and live the life of a child.

The family living in the house the other side of us had a daughter about the same age as me. Emily was very kind to me. We would often talk through the wooden fence that separated our two gardens. Most summer days she would be out in the sunshine playing with her toys however as the days went by she never appeared so I asked her mum if her daughter had gone away on vacation.

"Oh no, dear," she said. "My daughter has an infection that is highly contagious called impetigo." She went on to explain all about it. Here was the answer that I had been looking for! After all who would want a kid covered in sores from head to foot?

I knew that catching impetigo was going to keep me safe and away from the uncles that often came calling to my house. I made a plan of action and set to carry it out. Every Sunday morning Mr. and Mrs. Jones together with their sweet daughter Emily dressed in their finest clothes and off they would go for a couple of hours. Mrs. Jones had often talked with me through the garden fence about a man they go to be with every Sunday morning. She told me His name is Jesus. She said He loves us so very much. Often I would be in my back garden when Mrs. Jones came out to read a story to Emily from a very old and somewhat worn out book. I would sit as close to my side of the fence as possible so that I could hear every word. Her voice was so gentle and soothing and her stories so full of life that I found myself at peace within a heart so full of fear. I watched and waited for Sunday to arrive. While looking out of my front window early one morning I saw Mr. and Mrs. Jones walking away from their garden gate without Emily. Here was my opportunity! I had made a get-well picture for Emily and went around to her back door and knocked. I heard Emily ask, "Who's there?"

I said, "It's me! I made a picture for you."

"Come in," Emily said, so I went in and found Emily sitting on a bright orange couch. She looked so poorly. I sat on a huge dark green chair but still too far away from her. I knew I had to gain her trust to allow me to move closer, so I asked about the many bright red sores on her face. Emily told me she had them in most places over her body. My heart jumped with delight. But the reason I was there was not primarily to visit my sick friend but to help myself to those yucky sores on her face. Some of the sores had popped and formed a yellow crust on her now not so pretty face. "Perfect answer," I told myself. I asked her lots of questions about her condition and she said the impetigo covered most of her body parts.

"Do they itch?" I asked.

"Yes," she said, "very much. My mummy said not to touch them because that makes them spread."

"How long will you have them?" I asked. Emily started to cry so I changed the subject and talked about happy things and soon I had her laughing again. I asked if there was anything that I could do for her before I left.

"Would you please come closer and scratch my back? It is so itchy." I could not suppress the big smile that spread across my face. I did as requested, making sure that I contaminated myself. A little while later with a fever and swollen glands I knew that my mission had been a complete success. Soon my face looked just as yucky as Emily's did. I made sure that I infected every part of my body that I could reach and smiled that maybe one day I would be a contortionist. Being a smart little button I soon found ways to keep the impetigo active on most parts of my skin.

It was about this time that my daddy decided

he had enough of long-distance truck driving and found work at a local store so that he could be home with us every evening. Now it was time for me to heal both physically and mentally. My daddy was my hero and when he was not working we were inseparable. Peace reigned in our home once more and soon our family grew from two children to five children, adding two brothers and a cute little baby sister. Mother and Father both worked, Daddy by day, Mother by night, so a lot of the time I was caring for my younger siblings because Mother had to sleep during the day. Our grandma who still lived next door would pop in every once in a while to check all was well.

I remember one night mother was not working. My siblings and I were upstairs getting ready for bed. We shared a very large bed with girls at the top, boys at the bottom. I could hear mother shouting at daddy but I couldn't make out what she was saying. The next day when I came downstairs my daddy was sad. I walked over to his chair and laid my head on his shoulder. Slowly he put his arm around me and said, "Good morning, little one," but his voice was sad. Mother was nowhere to be seen. Daddy took all us kids out to the park and then for ice cream. Sure was so much fun. I liked that my daddy was home and taking care of us, but it wasn't to last.

I had attended school on and off, mostly off. These were days I hated. I had missed so much schooling with the impetigo and then I had head lice for what seemed like forever so in school I had no idea what was going on. I would sit at my desk by the window and stare off into space sometimes falling asleep and only waking when the school bell rang for recess or lunch. No one seemed to mind that I could not do school work or homework for that matter. Weeks and months came and went. Still I could not read or even write my own name.

Daddy and Mother would fight most nights. I crept down the stairs one night to listen and found out that my daddy had a big gambling problem and had lost his weeks' wage. Mother was in a rage letting him know that she was going to take care of things from now on. She told him to GET OUT!!

Saying goodbye to my daddy once again was not easy for me. He was my everything and I was his. Mother was true to her word and started working nights again. I can see her now. She had called me into her bedroom to help close the zipper on her dress. The dress was white with black polka dots all over it. It fit her full breast and tiny waist perfectly. With black high heels and her jet-black hair piled high on top of her head, she was a stunner for sure.

"You are to take care of the family tonight because I have to go to work," Mother told me. "No one is allowed in while I am gone. If your daddy comes here, you are NOT to let him in. Do you understand me?"

"Yes," was all I could say. I heard a car horn sound and she was gone. Daddy did come that night and yes I did let my daddy in. I needed to see him. I needed to talk to him. I needed to hear his voice and see his beautiful face and give him a hug. Yes, I knew there would be a punishment for disobeying Mother, but he was so well worth it to me. He stayed well into the evening and tried to explain what went wrong and why he could no longer live with us. I crawled up into his lap and as his arms surrounded me I laid my head on his chest and listened to his steady heartbeat, a heartbeat of complete contentment of a father holding the child that he loves. Suddenly the front door burst open with such a force that I jumped in fright. Mother and a stranger stood there looking at us. Mother took me by the wrist and marched me towards the stairs swinging my wrist so hard I thought for sure she would pull my arm out of place.

"GET UPSTAIRS!" she said through gritted teeth, and I did.

Voices from downstairs grew louder and my

heart raced with fear. Was my daddy ok? What was going on down there? I knew I had to help my daddy in some way but how? I could hear my daddy shouting, "Please stop!"

Our bedroom was at the back of the house so I went over to the window and opened it as wide as possible. I climbed out and along the window ledge, holding on for dear life. I climbed down the drainpipe into Mrs. Jones' back garden and banged on her door for help, overcome with fear. When Mr. Brown opened the door all I could say to him was, "They are killing my daddy! Please help us!" Mr. Brown called the police but by the time they came they found my daddy outside unconscious in our backyard. I don't remember much of what happened the rest of that night but in the morning when I came downstairs mother was waiting. The punishment she had for me did not fit the crime for a child not yet ten.

Mother stopped working nights and was home during the day too. During the warmer months I was told to take my siblings out to the park and when the lights came on in the park we could all come home. Most days a lunch of some kind was put together in a bag for us to enjoy. I have no idea what Mother did all day but by the time we came home the stranger was there. Mother decided it was time to tell us her plans so as we sat around the kitchen table eating oatmeal for supper mother told us we would all be moving to London. London? How far away is that? Would my daddy still be able to see us when he could? I was soon to find out for that tearful day was just around the corner. We all got busy downsizing our things and it wasn't long before Mother had one suitcase packed for each person. The stranger loaded all Mother gave him of our belongings into his small four-door car. No toys.

With four kids in the back seat and the adults and baby up front we were ready to go when out of the corner of my eye across the road stood my hero—my daddy. I climbed over my siblings to get out of the car through the open windows and I would have made it but Mother reached over, took hold of my ankle then shouted, "DRIVE!" and my hero was gone. London was too far for my daddy to come visit and too far for me to walk back to see him. I knew deep in my heart that it would be a very long time before I saw my daddy again.

Time for me to grow up and make the best of my situation, but where do I start?

The new stranger became Mother's boyfriend and things seemed to work out well. A new brother was added to the family only to be taken to heaven eight months later. Mother moved us all away and decided to live alone once more. We moved several times as a family from halfway house to halfway house. Then the government gave Mother an apartment for us all. Mother was soon out again in the evenings, but now I knew it was not for working nights cleaning offices like before. She got herself into some trouble that resulted in us four youngest children being taken away. My three younger siblings and I were taken to a govern-ment children's home in Essex. Due to the difference in our ages I was not allowed to be with my younger siblings in the home that was to be theirs for the remainder of their stay. I was still able to see them every day but my "home" was at the very top of a long driveway and theirs way at the bottom. My two brothers who were very close in age stayed together playing and hanging out. My baby sister would cry for me and didn't sleep well. I remember on one occasion the house parents let me stay over for the night and sleep with my baby sister. That was the best night's sleep each of us experienced. She lay in my arms as I gently stroked her hair and sang her song after song until she was fast asleep. In the morning she was there looking up at me with the biggest smile on her cute little pink face. Oh how I loved her!

Time passed and one day a social worker came

to inform me that I was going to be fostered out. I had no idea what that meant. I asked her if my siblings were coming with me and she said no. This was going to be the first time in my life that I would not be with them. Not available if they needed to talk. Not there if they needed a hug. Not there, period. I told the social worker that I was not going to go with her but I soon realized I had no choice. I was not even given time to say goodbye because of the emotional stress it would cause them, I was told later. With no time to say my goodbyes I became scared and made up my mind that I would do everything in my power to get back and be with my siblings as soon as I could.

COME WALK WITH ME

Chapter Three
NOBODY'S CHILD

The three months I spent as a foster child was a nightmare both for the foster parents and for me. They tried to love me as if I were their own. I didn't make it easy for them. They were of retirement age with no children of their own and here comes this wild child approaching her teen years. My mind was set on one thing; to do whatever it took to get back to my siblings. Little did I know that my negative behavior would only send me further away from those I loved.

Sure enough the day came when the social worker who had brought me to this loving couple came and took me away. I didn't care for any goodbyes this time. I just wanted to be out of there. Still angry, still confused, still wanting to be with my siblings but no, that was not going to be the case. I kept asking about my mother and my siblings, but she would not tell me anything as to their whereabouts. I asked the social worker if she would contact my daddy and she told me that my mother was given full custody. He had no access to us anymore.

Now I was really mad! What did she know about my family? We were just a case number on a file that she had in her hands at that time. I wanted to tell her about my younger siblings and how I needed to get back to them, how they depended on me, how I missed them so, how I needed to hug my baby sister and reassure her all would be ok. She didn't appear to care. She never once asked me about my family. We drove in silence to the east end of London where to my horror we stopped in front of a very old, very cold looking, dark brick building. I was marched up the white stone steps pulled by the sleeve of my jacket. Two heavy wooden doors squealed like a pig as they opened. My heart raced in fear as we entered. It was a children's home for naughty girls. They had a place waiting for me. I was led to a bench in the hallway, set down firmly and told not to move while the social worker and the staff talked behind closed doors. Once office formalities were completed the social worker left without a word, a wave goodbye, or even so much as a wish for luck.

I was trapped! I sat there in the reception area all alone for what seemed like forever not knowing where to go or what to do. As the sunlight dimmed and the shadows lengthened into scary shapes a rather tiny lady appeared and stood right in front of me. My first thought was she was one of the girls, but no, she was the matron, the boss lady, the one that I wanted to stay on the right side of if I wanted to see my siblings again. So with the sweetest voice I could render I introduced myself. She leaned forward not saying a word and stared at me through gold-rimmed glasses perched on the end of her cute tiny nose.

"Hmm, you will do nicely," she said in her strange cockney accent. Then she took my hand and led me into the dining room where I sat with about one hundred girls of different ages and colors. Everyone looked at me. No one talked to me. Then Matron, as she was always called, told the girls my name and left the room.

That night I cried myself to sleep thinking about my little siblings, Mother and Daddy.

I had never seen a dormitory before. Ten beds

lined the walls on either side of the room. A small dark brown unit separated each bed from the next and held the personal effects of the occupier. It was a no-no to touch what was not yours. We were all given weekly work to do. I had to keep my own personal space spic and span if I wanted to eat that day. I was assigned to clean bathrooms— five large bathrooms on the top level of this home.

I liked to clean. While I was cleaning I lost myself in a world of childhood memories, times when Daddy and I would go to the beach and play in the sand. Times when he would talk for what seemed like hours to the many fishermen that lined the sandy beachfront repairing their nets ready for the next big catch. I would sit and listen to stories tall and small, laughing when they laughed without really under-standing why. It was on one of those days when Daddy and I went to the beach that he had to go see a friend and asked the fishermen to keep an eye on me. He told me he would be back in an hour or so and to stay with the fishermen until he returned— and then he was gone. I started to build a good-sized sand-castle, collecting lots of different shells to divide the many rooms inside. I found lots of dark green seaweed to decorate with. Often the fishermen would look my way and smile and I smiled back. One gave me an empty can that I used to make four towers on the very top of my sandcastle and then I stood back to admire my work of art. I sat beside my castle and looked out to sea. How very peaceful the ocean blue looked with its soft white waves gently rolling in to shore. As I laid my head down on the warm golden sand the voices of the fishermen faded as I drifted into a deep and peaceful sleep. I woke up feeling cold and hungry. It was beginning to get dark and still Daddy had not returned. The fishermen were putting away their day's work and getting ready to go home. I walked over to them to ask if my daddy had come back yet. "No, child," was the reply. Fear gripped my heart. Where was my daddy? I knew he would not abandon me, he loved me too much. Yet it seemed he had done just that. The older fisherman came over to where I was sitting by my sandcastle and asked if he could walk me home. He had a kind face.

"It will be dark soon and not safe for you to stay on the beach alone."

I had to make a decision. I placed my tiny hand in his large brown weathered hand and together we walked silently side by side to my house. Waiting at the front door was Mother. The two exchanged words briefly then she led me by my wrist into the kitchen.

"Your precious daddy is in the hospital," is all I

heard before I hit the floor from a mighty blow across my head from a very angry fist.

A bell sounded bringing me back to reality and once again sadness filled my heart as the pain of my lost family took its toll on my emotions.

Most if not all of the girls in care with me were there as wards of the court. However, I was not, therefore I was able to go out alone. I did this most afternoons to explore my new surroundings. I soon found making friends was not as difficult as I first thought it would be. An elderly couple ran the sweet candy and tobacco store at the end of the road. Most days I would visit there and we would chat for a while. I had no money to buy anything but that didn't seem to matter to them. I felt very welcome and sometimes they gave me a small treat just for stopping in. Over the months I grew to love this dear old couple. They were so down to earth in every way. Teasing each other in front of me had us all in fits of uncontrollable laughter. Now this would be a family I could call my own.

The next day after my chores were completed I was getting ready to go out when a very large, very strong girl approached me and gripped me firmly on my shoulder. I flinched in pain. She told me to come back with cigarettes for her or I would be very sorry. I knew what I must do, what I should do, what I was going to do— TELL!! But not the staff of the children's home, oh no that would lead to more trouble for me. I was going to tell the only couple that I had come to trust and respect but most of all... love. They both listened intently as I shared my conversation with the girl at the home. As he took his white wrinkled hand down from his chin I saw a smile spread across his sweet face.

"No problem," he said as he turned to look at his wife who by now was also smiling and seemed to fully understand her husband's thoughts. What were they up to? I didn't take anything away with me this visit except a happy feeling that I had someone on my side. The next day was Sunday and Matron was on duty. All the supper dishes had been put away and all of us were upstairs getting ready for bed. Matron had gone back downstairs to watch her T.V. program. I was brushing my teeth when I was grabbed from behind and forced over to one of the five old stone bathtubs that filled this room. Face to face with my enemy she said, "This is a warning." Then I was pushed down into very cold water with many hands too strong to fight off. I could see the many faces looking down at me, faces laughing, not caring the outcome of this situation. I tried to hold my breath as long as I could but my air was gone and my life would soon follow.

I woke up in the hospital with no one to talk to. The small room was as white as snow, very white, sheets and walls, even the bedside chair. My bed was the only one in this room. I waited, not daring to move in case it hurt. The door opened and in walked Matron with flowers for me. She put the flowers in a vase next to my bed and sat down facing me. She told me what had happened and ended by warning me if I tell anyone I would never see the dear old couple again. The door opened again and in walked a man dressed in white.

"You ready to go home?"

Home? Where was my home? All I could think about was the kind old couple who had made many of my days, happy ones. Yes, I was ready to go home, ready to go and visit them once more. They would become my home. I returned with Matron to the children's home and peace reigned once again. Over the next couple of months, I made a plan to visit the candy shop every day except Sunday. A strong loving bond was growing between the three of us. On one of those visits they asked me if I would like to be part of their family permanently. We held on to each other, crying for joy. I couldn't wait to ask Matron if this would be possible so as soon as I saw her in the dining room I asked her and everyone nearby heard me. That was a big mistake on my part because now my enemy had another opportunity to get hold of me and make her request known. That evening she told me all that she wanted from the candy store. I told her I would bring her back a treat and she seemed happy with my answer. The next day while at the candy store we put together a plan of action. I was instructed how to carry out this plan and smiled as my mind rehearsed the moves I would make to insure my enemy would not win. That night while waiting in line for the toilet she was standing behind me hitting me in the back and pulling my hair, her final acts of amusement. When it was my turn I pretended to go, while she was banging on the door to hurry me along. I had a tube of what today is called super glue. I carefully smeared it all around the seat and counted to ten. Pushing me out of the way she sat her big bottom down firmly and exploded while leaving the door wide open so she could scream negative and hateful words at me. I slowly backed away from the toilet door keeping my eyes fastened on hers and waited. She rested her arms on her legs contemplating her next move, glaring at me with eyes that said, "I'm gonna get you for sure." I stood very still and very straight. A smile slowly crept across my face. Had it worked? Was she bonded with the seat? It took five firemen to free her AND the toilet seat (which was now part of her) from the toilet. She was placed tummy down or should I say bottom up on a stretcher and taken to the hospital. (I guess she will always have a ring of confidence!)

The next day I was moved to another children's home on the other side of London. They said it was for my own safety. I never saw my candy couple again yet their love and acceptance of me will always serve as a reminder that there are kind people in this world if I'm willing to look for them. My new place of residence was very new and up to date. One male director, two male staff, and two female staff ran the home. Only ten girls were living there at the time I moved in. Everyone seemed pleased to have me join this family and after a lovely dinner of fish and chips the director asked the girls which room I should be placed in. Well, I had never had others fight over me before wanting me to share their room. This was new to me. I smiled as a feeling of worth took hold of my heart and for once I allowed myself to be pulled in the direction of my new bedroom. Two beds with matching covers and curtains made this room a sweet delight. Two dressers, two chairs and a big mirror completed the look of "home."

I had never had much schooling and still didn't know how to read but my roommate who was an A student read to me most nights. I would never hear the end of her stories because her soft voice would always put me to sleep. She had been placed there after the passing of her grandma who had raised her. Inside this home the girls were given opportunity for education. It was a choice not forced on anyone but made to be exciting with hands-on activities like cooking, sewing or crafts. One of the hobbies offered was music. How I loved music! I loved to sing, loved to dance, loved the way music made me feel on the inside. Our piano music teacher was not a member of staff full time but a substitute when needed. He volunteered to give us lessons for free so I signed up. The piano teacher sat on the stool with me and smiled when he said, "Every time you make a mistake by hitting the wrong key I will touch you and make you laugh." He touched me several times but I was not laughing, I was frightened.

A little while later he was covering night duty for a full-time staff member that was sick. My bed was the first one inside the door and the other was by the window. As always I fell asleep before the end of the story but this night I woke to find I was not the only person in my bed. Hands moved over my body as a voice quietly said, "Keep still." I lay there unable to move, unable to breathe, unable to cry out for help, remembering back and thinking, "Not again." The next night I asked my roommate if I could sleep by the window because I was too hot in my bed. She said, "Yes." This time I heard the story all the way to the end. I heard her turn off the light. I heard the bedroom door open and close, and then I heard her scream. Oh boy, did she scream! Staff and girls came running and he was taken to jail.

My roommate and I remained good friends until my sixteenth birthday when I told the director that I was leaving to go find my family. That was my next mission.

The director gave me a train ticket and an address where I could find Mother. Traveling blind I knew there would be obstacles to overcome but there was no turning back now. I would find Mother, my siblings and Daddy and we would be a family once more.

COME WALK WITH ME

Chapter Four
A REUNION OF SORTS

The train ride was full of lovely scenery the further away from London we got. A lady that shared my cabin on the train asked me where I was going so I handed her the address that the director had written down for me on a piece of paper. "Oh my," she said, as she placed her right hand on her heart. "I am going to visit my daughter who lives on the very same road. You and I can share the journey together." And share we did only I got out of the taxi first and she continued on up the road. Now I stood at the gate leading to the house. Behind those doors was the beginning to the end of my long wait. My heart was pumping so loudly I was sure the whole road could hear it. I walked up the pathway and knocked on the door. I heard footsteps coming closer and then the door opened wide. There stood Mother as beautiful as I remembered. Dark hair piled high on her head, long pants and a tight fitted shirt showed she had not lost her looks. With the warmest of smiles, she said, "May I help you?"

I couldn't talk. I opened my mouth but no words came out.

"Are you all right dear?"

I just wanted to take in this sight. Face to face with Mother after so many years apart but she had no idea who I was. Should I tell her? How do you introduce yourself to your own mother? What words would be the very first she would want to hear from her own child after so long? She stood there waiting, "Hello, Mother. It's me, your daughter. I have come home to be with you."

Her face drained of all color. I thought she was going to pass out from the shock. Once she composed herself her reply was the last words I thought I would ever hear coming out of my own mother's mouth. Looking straight at me she said, "I don't want you! I have never wanted you! You, young lady, will

NEVER amount to anything," and she closed the door in my face.

I stood there for what seemed an eternity staring at the closed door. Was I dreaming? Had I really knocked on that door and got an answer I didn't expect. I can't describe to you in adequate words the state of my heart, my mind, my emotions were raw. Why does she hate me so much? Why does she not want me after all these years? Why am I not good enough for her? Why? Why? Now what was I to do? I still had some money in my pocket so I picked up my small suitcase and headed in the direction of the main town. I found a coffee shop and sat down to think through what had just happened to me. The waitress came over, took one look at my face and knew I was in trouble. She came back with a glass of milk and some toast. "Stay here and wait for me to finish my shift, then we will talk." I did just that. She took me home with her that night and made me a bed on the couch. The next morning, we sat at her kitchen table to talk through what options I had. None seemed like family. The only answer she knew was to contact the children's services. They came and took me to a children's home.

Mothers of the Order of God ran the home. I shared a room with a red head girl about my age. Since I still could not read she and I decided that I would do her share of the household chores and she would go out to work then share her income with me. This arrangement worked out really well and one evening we were allowed to go out together but curfew was ten sharp. Dressed to kill, we set out for the evening and made our way to the fun fair. It wasn't long before my friend saw a young man that took her fancy and she asked me to help her get him.

"No problem," I said and before the hour was over the two guys treated us to ice cream. The guy she liked was fond of me. He held my hand and said he would like to see me again. My roommate was not happy with me!

We arrived back to the nuns' home on the stroke of ten. Once we were in our room she took her bed pillow and standing on her bed hit me with her pillow. So I followed suit hitting her with all my might and receiving back the same. Our pillows suddenly burst open and millions of tiny white feathers drifted like snowflakes to the ground. We did look a sight holding empty pillowcases and covered in tiny white feathers! We burst into laughter and fell on our beds. The door opened and in walked Mother Superior and a sister holding "the rod of correction." In a very soft voice we were told we had one hour to clean up this mess and that for every feather found we would each receive a tasting from the rod of correction. Well, we moved like the wind picking up every feather we could see. They were everywhere, now they were contained inside the pillowcases and placed back on each bed. True to her word in she came wearing gloves and inspected our room hoping to find a reason to administer the said punishment. Not one feather did she find. As she was leaving our room she said we were both grounded until further notice and closed the door. The wind must have caught the door as it closed because one small white feather came sailing down from the ledge above the door. We looked at each other and grinned.

Time passed and the home returned to normal. The girls were not required to follow in the footsteps of their caregivers but I must say a peace rested over me the entire time I was living in that home.

One afternoon I was called into the office and told to put all my things in my suitcase because I was moving. I tried to ask questions to find out more information but was quickly shown the door. Where was I going this time? Would I go back to London? I was full of questions. The sister escorted me to the waiting area and stayed with me until a car arrived. At first I couldn't see who was in the car but once I was eye level my heart left my chest in pure delight. Sitting in the back seat of the car were my three younger siblings and up front mother and her new husband. I didn't care about that, I just wanted to be a family again, to have and to hold my own siblings and kiss them and hug them and be a big sister the best I knew how. Stepfather drove us out into the country to a lovely three-bedroom house. Trees covered the back yard and rosebushes the front. A gravel pathway went all the way around the house, our house, our own home!

Time for me to grow up and get a job and that is just what I did— working as a junior welder. I quickly learned to meet each day's quota. One day a spark burned through my skirt and burned my upper thigh. I was taken home to find only my stepfather was in the house. He got the medicine box and a small stool from the kitchen and sat down in front of me to dress my wound. He elevated my leg to rest on his knee and applied medicine to the burnt area just as Mother and the kids came home. She fixed dinner and soon we were all sitting around the table as a family once again. The leg healed and I returned to work, happy to be back with good friends.

Mother started to get sick and was not able to cope. The doctors decided she needed to go away for a time of rest so my stepfather took care of us for the months that followed. Because mother was placed in a facility close by my stepfather was able to visit her often. No children were allowed, or so he told us.

One night when I came home from work he was taking care of my younger siblings so I went to take a bath. Soaking in bubbles up to my neck I never heard the bathroom door open but there my stepfather stood urinating into the toilet right in front of me. As he was finishing up he turned to me and said, "Tonight you will share my bed," and he left. No way! I shared my bed with my siblings and only my siblings. Never again would I let anyone use me for his own pleasure. It was time for a plan of action, but what?

Stepfather had gone to visit Mother and would be back as soon as it got dark. I fed and bathed my siblings and told them a made-up story before kissing them all good night. I had a plan of action; now to be brave enough to carry it out. It's one thing to say but totally different to do. I looked in the knife drawer and found the biggest and sharpest knife I could find. My heart was already beating so fast; could I do this? I sat on the stairs leading up to the bedrooms. Gripping the knife tightly in both hands I had to convince myself I only had one chance to make it count. I knew nothing about stabbing a person, let alone a family member. As I sat there thinking things through I heard the front garden gate open and shut. He was on his way. Had I remembered to lock the back kitchen door so he would have to enter the house through the front door? I put the knife on the step above me. I crawled on all fours, racing for the back door. Yes, it was locked. Now to get back in place and ready to strike. I heard more than one voice outside my front door. Who was there? Would they be able to help protect me? I stumbled to the front door and turned the key flinging the door open wide. When my eyes adjusted to the dark, I saw three people standing there and one of them was the guy I had met at the fun fair all those months ago. Still firmly gripping the sharp knife in my right hand all I could say was, "He is going to die! He is going to die!"

David, Mike and his girlfriend Sandy came into the house and after Sandy made a cup of tea for everyone, I told them what my stepfather had said to me before he went out. David was not happy to hear this and said that he would wait for my stepfather to return home so that he could speak with him. I felt so relieved and started to calm down. David took the knife from the counter and placed it back in the kitchen drawer. We all heard the front gate open and close. We all heard the footsteps on the gravel coming closer to the front door. David gently reached out and placed his hand on my arm and with a smile said, "It will be ok."

My stepfather came into the room smelling of beer. He shouted at me and asked what was going on. David took him by the arm, led him into the family room and closed the door. There was no more shouting in fact I could not hear a thing so I went out the back door and around to the front window that was slightly open. I could hear and see them both.

David had my stepfather up against the wall with only one hand. I looked on the scene in absolute delight! Then I heard David tell my stepfather that he was going to marry me. David made it very clear that if my stepfather valued his life he would never say or do anything to scare me or hurt me. David told him that from this day on we were boyfriend and girlfriend and that this relationship would lead to marriage within a year. I begged David not to leave me but he assured me that all would be well and that he would return next weekend and every weekend until we were married. He kept true to his word.

David took time on the weekends to teach me how to read and write my own name. He was so patient and so kind. Over and over again I would write my maiden name and then my new married name until I was confident and could write both with my eyes closed. I would write it in all sorts of textures. When we would go out to eat I would "spill" liquid on the tabletop just so I could write my name for him to read. This made him smile with deep love and devotion. At the beach I wrote in the sand and he chuckled at my sweetness as I danced about with joy. We were so much in love.

October 31, 1969 David and I were married. We had a wedding full of close friends and family, a wedding that told me I was valued, I was loved and I was safe and protected. I was married to a man who filled my heart to overflowing with his tenderness and unconditional love.

Three years passed and as I turned twenty David and I decided we would try to add to our family. Within a short time, I found out we were pregnant. David was over the moon! Being three weeks late for a child you have waited nine months for was getting too much for me so it was decided to induce labor and four hours later my husband was holding his princess safely in his arms. As we made our way home, David carried our baby in his arms stopping every person he knew to show off his princess. Cordelia Jayne, our daughter, was our pride and joy. Having very little experience as parents it was learn-as-you-go. I often look back and wonder how our daughter ever made it to one-year-old. By the time Cordelia was four months I found out another baby was on the way. This baby was not planned yet it would be loved with all the love that we could give. Cordelia's brother also arrived three weeks late. Devlin Stacey completed our little family.

Dee as she was called liked her little brother very much. At his bath times we would give her a little bath so she could bathe her baby doll while I was bathing Devlin. Dee would watch me then copy what I did. I would wash his hair, she would wash her doll's hair, I would sing to Devlin she would sing to her baby. When it came to feeding time I made sure there was a small baby doll bottle so she could feed her baby while I nursed mine. Those were happy days. David would often get home from work well before the children went to bed so that he could play with them and speak into their hearts just how much he loved them. One day I was getting the children ready to go to town to meet my mother for the first time. She had moved into the area and asked if she could see her grandchildren. We had planned to meet at one o'clock in the local coffee shop in town. I went upstairs to get the baby ready and never once thought this day would be one of the saddest days of my life. I picked out his very best outfit and laid it on my bed. I had everything ready so I went into his room and opened the curtains then turned around to look at him. I instantly knew something was wrong. I moved closer to his crib. He was lying very still. I watched for any sign of movement to indicate he was breathing... nothing. I felt sick. I felt cold. I felt pain I had never felt before. I gently picked up my son to discover his life was gone. I laid him down and went to call the emergency services. The old ambulance man wrapped my son in his baby blanket and we ran to the ambulance together. My neighbor who heard the siren came and took care of Dee.

"Will my son be ok?" I asked him. The old man with tears in his eyes kept looking at my son and said, "He is in the arms of Jesus now. I had no idea what he meant.

We arrived at the hospital where my son was born only eight weeks earlier. Devlin was laid on a bed. The young doctor said my son had already passed away. In a fit of rage, I hit the doctor so hard that he hit his head against the sink and was out cold. I screamed at the top of my lungs for help. A nurse came running and put a shot into my arm. I was out cold. Mother would never meet her first grandson.

When I woke up David was sitting beside my bed still wearing his work clothes, his eyes swollen and red from the many tears he had shed over the loss of his son. I looked at him and said, "I'm so very sorry for losing your son." Tears of pain and shame fell freely from my eyes. He leaned forward to kiss me on top of my head and held me while I sobbed into his chest. David wrapped his loving arm around my shoulders as we walked home through the town but this time he never spoke to a single soul. We were wrapped up in our pain that no one else could feel, a pain so strong no medicine could heal. As we got closer to the house the horror of the day replayed in my mind. I didn't want to go inside the house. I didn't want to see the clean clothes I had laid out on my bed for him to wear to meet his grandma for the first time. I didn't want to see his baby bath still waiting to be used or the crib that held his lifeless body.

Dee's voice broke my thoughts. I turned to see her running down the pathway of my neighbor's garden to greet me. She was such a beautiful child, so full of smiles, so full of fun, so full of life. David picked Dee up and held her tightly in his arms burying his face in her tiny neck. "That tickles, Daddy!" she said laughing. Dee was our medicine. Dee was our future. Dee was our hope to survive. Once inside the house I noticed that all of Devlin's things were gone. I was told much later that Dee's caregiver had put all of his things in her basement until I wanted them back. How thoughtful, how kind.

Dee became our everything. Each day this child helped to heal our hearts with her childlike ways. David returned to work and Dee and I began a new life together doing happy things each day. It was bath time for Dee and as I got things ready she asked if Devlin was going to get a bath too. I held back my emotions rising inside. This precious child was too young to understand her brother was now in heaven and would never take a bath with us again. Devlin was with God, so the preacher said at his funeral. I sat there cold as ice. Nothing he said made any sense to me. Who was this so-called God of love anyway? Why did He allow my son to die? What had my son ever done to Him? Was I being punished? If so, for what? Why punish an innocent child for the sins of the parents? I just don't get it! Dee continued to ask questions about her baby brother and over time I felt myself slipping into a depression so black I could not cope with even the simplest task. David tried to carry on as best he could. He put Dee with a babysitter during the day and brought her home at six with him. I was told much later it was six months before I was able to be a mother and wife again. David and Dee took great care of me and the healing of the heart was well on the mend. I went to see our family doctor for a checkup and was told we were pregnant once again.

Life was getting back to a normal happy one as my tummy grew with our love child safely inside. I can remember one Saturday evening David, Dee and I were sitting on the couch laughing at a funny movie that had just finished on television. David made a cup of tea for me and juice for Dee and brought it to the couch where we were waiting. I placed the cup and saucer on my eight-month pregnant tummy. In no time at all, our love child kicked it off with one mighty kick and the cup and saucer flew into the air and landed on the floor in pieces. Dee was delighted and shouted, "Again, Daddy, again!" and so he did with every cup and saucer we had. To hear and see the laughter on her cute little face as she became animated with excitement was so worth the sacrifice of all those dishes. We laughed together until tears of joy ran down our faces. It was such good medicine for the soul.

Richard was born just like his other siblings— three weeks late. David and I cried at his birth, we had a son! I would not fail as a mother this time. I would not fail as a wife in protecting David and this new life. We brought a baby harness that strapped firmly to the parent allowing the child to be "connected" at all times to the caregiver. Everywhere I went Richard went. Everything I did he did too. For the first year of his little life we would be as one. We moved to another part of town and family life was normal once again.

Dee's fourth birthday was coming up and we decided to give her a big party at home. We invited many close friends to join in this celebration. The house was packed to overflowing with people of all ages. Party games were in full swing both inside and outside the house. I put the finishing touches to Dee's birthday cake and placed it on the brightly colored tablecloth in the kitchen. All was ready. Looking out of my small kitchen window I saw the game was coming to an end. I decided it was time to eat when all of a sudden I heard this very loud crash coming from the family room then everything went silent. I walked into the room to find David lying on the floor beside a smashed glass coffee table. Unaware of what had happened before I entered the room, I knelt down beside him and called his name. "David! David! Wake up," but he never answered me. I shook him firmly more than once but he never said ouch. He was still. I ran to the phone and dialed the emergency services for help. There was movement behind me as all the adults had the children file out the back door. I came along side my husband and kneeling down placed my head on his chest to listen for his heartbeat... nothing. The emergency services arrived and took him away. I remember watching them put David on a stretcher. I remember them taking him out the front door of the home we shared as man and wife. I remember seeing our family doctor enter through that same door and sit beside me on the couch. He took me in his arms and never said a word.

I can't tell you where Dee or Richard went. I can't tell you what happened to the birthday party. I can't tell you who cleaned up. All I can tell you is this, my world, my life, my love, my husband would never be coming home again. David was given a military funeral because he was still enlisted in the army part time. The tiny church was packed with men in uniform with brass buttons that shone like the sun and in contrast ladies in black. I sat there like before cold as ice, Dee on one side of me, Richard on the other. A light luncheon was provided following the service and then home once again. This time without the support of the man I loved.

COME WALK WITH ME

Chapter Five
NEW BEGINNINGS

At home with my two children I took them into my arms and held their tiny bodies close to mine. These were the children David and I had made together, conceived in love. Now they only had me to love, feed, protect and keep them safe. Only me. I tried to do the best I knew how yet I felt so alone. Letters and bills started to arrive. David had taken care of these because I still could not read very well, but he was not here anymore. As the days turned into weeks the reality of bereavement took a firm hold on my emotions. I tried to make sense of life without my man beside me. Our children deserved the best. What was the best? What could I give our children that would even come close to all they had lost in their short lives on earth? What?

Our friends phoned every now and then to ask how things were and if there was anything we needed. I wanted to scream and say, "YES, WE WANT DAVID BACK!" But I controlled myself and said we were doing just fine. Soon the phone calls stopped. Friends stopped coming by. My life was turning black. I could not cope with the everyday needs of our children. I cried. I tried to close out the darkness and pain of loneliness.

It was about this time that my younger brother moved into the area and came to visit with his girlfriend. I liked Carole from the first time we met and before long she moved in with the children and me. Carole was just what I needed to get even with God. After all, this so-called God of love had taken from me that which I loved the most, my firstborn son and my husband. I found out from a visiting preacher what hurt God the most— sin. Sin hurt God— doing what is wrong. Here was my plan of action: to sin the best I knew. During the months that followed I allowed myself to live in Satan's camp, to do everything I knew to do wrong, to hurt God like He had hurt me. I was going to get even no matter what it took. As the months went by the only person hurting was I. I fell deeper and deeper into a pit. Pain I had never known gripped my heart as I realized I had become the scum of the earth. Now I know God was hurting too: hurting to see the pain I was in, hurting to see me held in bondage by the lies I believed from the mouth of Satan. God wanted to help me but He was waiting for my invitation, an invitation that would come through the prayers of another.

Carole moved away after her marriage to my brother and I was alone once more. Depression firmly set in. My sweet children deserved the love and support of two parents, not just one. One night after tucking them in bed and kissing them both goodnight, I went into the bathroom. The medicine cupboard was full of brightly colored pills that had been stored there over time. I took these down to the kitchen and poured all of them into a cereal bowl. Here was the answer to end my loneliness. The bowl was full to the top; all I had to do was empty it into my tummy and go to sleep forever. I was only thinking of me, my pain, me, me, me.

Someone was knocking at my door. Who could it be? I didn't have many people come calling any more. I opened the front door to see a kind face looking back at me. He told me he was a social worker and asked if he may come in and chat awhile. Graham followed me into the kitchen and sat at my kitchen table while I made us both a cup of tea. He never said a word about all the pills that sat right in front of him. He asked how the children were doing so I took him upstairs to see them. Both were fast asleep cuddling their soft toys. Graham had a soft voice that was tender towards me. He said he would arrange for help Monday through Friday for the daily care of the children. He spoke of assistance through government programs. He asked if I needed help right then. I showed him mountains of letters and bills that had arrived since David had passed away. I also told him that I couldn't read. Graham had the brightest blue eyes I had ever seen. His smile was so real, so happy, so full of life. He asked me if I would like to learn to read but that was not part of my plan. "I don't know," was my answer.

Graham told me he could arrange for a lady from his church to teach me to read while the children were being cared for. He seemed to have all the answers. Then he said something that sent my blood to the boiling point.

"God loves you."

I saw red. I kicked back my chair as I lurched at

his face, my clenched fist catching his lip with my ring and drawing blood. He stood as we got down and dirty, each fighting for different reasons. He held on to this wild child for dear life as I bit, kicked and punched him anywhere and everywhere I could. He started to speak out loud in words that made no sense. He got louder and louder all the while holding me tightly in a bear hug.

Suddenly I stopped fighting. We sank to the floor still holding on to each other. My head was resting against his chest. I wondered how long we had been in this fight since it was now dark outside, when all of a sudden a light came through my kitchen window right towards us. This powerful light outshone the darkness as it came to rest where we were kneeling. Graham gently released his grip on me and leaned back as the light penetrated the space between us and entered my heart of stone breaking the chains of death that had held me bound for far too long. I heard and felt a snap around my heart. Graham gently lifted my chin just as the breath of Christ gave me my first breath of eternal life. I was set free. Graham said my face shone with the glory of the Lord as he helped me to my feet.

"What just happened to me?" I asked him.

"You are now a child of the King," he said smiling. "Welcome to God's family." Graham read to me from the Bible he carried in his briefcase.

The Gospel of John, chapter three verse sixteen "FOR GOD SO LOVED THE WORLD THAT HE GAVE HIS ONLY BEGOTTEN SON THAT WHO-EVER BELIEVES IN HIM WILL NOT PERISH BUT HAVE EVERLASTING LIFE."

Graham smiled at me and read it again only this time he made it personal. "FOR GOD SO LOVED ELLY THAT HE GAVE HIS ONLY SON, JESUS, THAT IF ELLY BELIEVES IN JESUS, ELLY WILL NOT DIE BUT HAVE EVERLASTING LIFE." "God so loved Elly" kept repeating over and over in my head. After all that I did wrong, all that I did to hurt God, He still loved me. Graham stayed awhile longer and shared powerful stories of lives changed by the power of a loving and gracious God. I took in every word he said. These words filled my heart with hope. This was a new beginning for me.

Graham arranged with a lady from his church who was an English teacher to teach me to read. Hillary had two small sons of her own yet still found time to be my teacher and friend. My reading book was the Bible. I can't remember how many times I would throw it across her living room in frustration.

"Hil" as I called her, would smile at me and say, "When you're ready, go pick it up and we will begin again." This dear soul had the patience of a saint and during that year became the first Christian friend I grew to trust and love. She will always be part of my story because she never gave up on me. I know she prayed daily for me and still does I'm sure.

Graham and his lovely wife Heather became my spiritual parents. I grew in knowledge of the Holy Scriptures the weekends that my children and I spent at their home in the country. They would have daily devotions with us and explain so that we understood what God was saying through His word. I loved being with them because they were so full of the love of God. Their two sons became big brothers to my children and together we shared in many hours of family fun. Heather was gifted at the piano and played choruses for us to sing. "Somewhere in Outer Space" was my favorite song. It talked about God preparing a place for those that love Him and trust Him. It said Jesus will come again and that the countdown is getting lower every day.

Every night as I put my children to bed we would sing this song while climbing the stairs because it has counting in it.

"Ten and nine, eight and seven, six and five and four.
Call upon the Savior while you may.

Three and two coming through the clouds in bright array.
The countdown is getting lower every day."

Prayer time included thanking Jesus for helping us to be a happy family once again. I continued to ride with Heather and Graham to church every Sunday morning and in the evening one of them would stay with my children at my house so I could go to the evening service. It was at one of the evening services that my emotions did a double summersault and feelings rose up in me that I had laid to rest with the death of David. Where did these feelings coming from? Standing by the youth pastor at the front of the church was a man I had to get to know, but why?

Johnathan had led this man to Christ many years ago when they were both patients in the same burns hospital. Alan had been invited by Johnathan to visit for the weekend and so here he was. Long dark black curly hair reached down past his shoulders. His trim body was covered with a heavy grey army trench coat. His bare feet had only flip-flops in the dead of winter. I smiled to myself thinking, "What do we have here?" After the service was finished I was introduced to Alan and we exchanged smiles. I asked him how long he would be staying and his reply took me back a bit. "As long as I want."

I tried a different approach, "When are you leaving?"

"When I'm ready." As he looked at me a smile crept across his face that got my blood boiling.

That week a young lady from church came to visit me and while she was at my house asked if she could use the telephone to call her "friend." I had no idea who her "friend" was. Her friend was Alan. In those days, caller ID displayed the caller's name and number so now Alan knew my phone number. I was not happy.

Alan was in church the following Sunday for both services but I made sure to stay as far away as possible from him. That week my friend came around again and used the phone to call her "friend". The next day, to my surprise, Alan called and said he would like to visit us. I told him he was not welcome unless he brought the youth pastor with him, which he did. Alan and Johnathan arrived Friday evening and Alan had toys for both of my children: a bright red truck for Richard and the prettiest doll for Dee she had ever seen. Alan removed his coat and lay on the floor playing with MY children. Johnathan and I sat watching not saying a word to each other. The next morning was Saturday so Dee, Richie, as I called him, and I went to town. As we walked down the street, Alan and Johnathan were walking on the other side of the road coming our way. Alan called out but I kept walking pulling my children along as fast as their little legs could run. Alan and Johnathan caught up and invited us to Sunday Tea at Johnathan's house the next day to which both kids said, "YES!!" Kids...

It was at Johnathan and Vera's home that Alan asked me to marry him. Talk about shock! I talked this over with Graham and Heather. I talked this over with Hil and Andy. I asked Johnathan and Vera for their input but most important, I asked Dee and Richie. "Yes and Amen!" was the answer I got from them all.

Alan and I were baptized three months later on the same day at the same location. Graham baptized me and Johnathan baptized Alan. Alan called us every night. He talked with the children until they were laughing so hard I had to rescue the phone. Every weekend he would come and visit and on September 1, 1979 we were married in the sight of God: married in the same church where we first met, married in the same church where we were baptized. "The two shall become one" were the words that pierced my heart with the greatest love I had ever felt for another human being since David. The road ahead of us would be filled with obstacles but we would overcome them together as a family, remaining faithful to God who made all this possible.

COME WALK WITH ME

Chapter Six
GOD'S GRACE REVEALED

Alan and I became very involved in church life. We soon discovered we were pregnant. True to form, Rebecca Anne was born three weeks late. We moved into town and purchased a house that was being sold by Hillary and Andy. Soon our fourth child, Matthew, was added to complete our family. Our new home was full of God's love. We opened it to the working young people in our church youth group and from noon until two in the afternoon we daily had fellowship and food together. This was one way that our four children could get to know the young people in our church family.

Rebecca and Matthew, who were too young for school, would wait at the front window until they heard a friendly "Hello" they recognized then would scramble to the door to greet the visitor with hugs and happy chatter. The older two, Dee and Richie, would join in as they could during school holidays. Val was the favorite lunchtime girlfriend of the children because she carried exciting Bible stories for them to listen to while she tried to eat her lunch. Robbie would arrive on the front courtyard with a "vroom, vroom" from his motorcycle. The young people loved our children and our children loved them right back. Alan and I made sure there was plenty to eat for those that "forgot" their lunches.

We heard about a Keith Green concert that was being held nearby so we decided to go as a couple. We should have got there much earlier because it was packed so we had to sit five seats apart. This was going to be a life changer for both of us. God was working in our hearts throughout the evening and as the "call to serve God" was given we both stood to our feet. We talked about our feelings all the way home. We talked about the call to serve with our church leadership and close friends. Alan and I prayed and wrote down scripture to see what God wanted of us. How would He have us serve? Where would He have us serve? We sent away for information on the needs of third world countries and Kenya answered the need first. In 1985 Alan went to East Africa with a team for four months and I stayed in England taking care of things. When he returned he was so full of the wonders and lifestyle of Mombasa, Kenya we both knew that we would one day return as a family. In 1986 our home church commissioned us to go to the mission field so with four suitcases and four children we went on an adventure of a lifetime. East Africa here we come! Mombasa would be our new home.

We soon made friends with the people Alan had met when he was there the year before. John Manzia shared a room with Alan during the 1985 visit and the two became best friends. Standing six-foot-tall and strong Manzia would carry our son Matthew on his shoulders and the two of them harmonized together singing, "Kaloo, how are you? How are you, John Kaloo?" At six in the morning the sun would rise to greet the new day. By six in the evening the sun said goodnight to the moon as they exchanged places. I remember one story Alan told us of the times they were together in the Shimba Hills. John Mangia was patrolling the compound when he heard a noise in the trees above. Putting his finger to his lips to silence everyone, John drew back his bow and arrow and shot into the treetop. With a thud a very large African skunk hit the ground dead.

Our adventures unfolded the more time we spent with our new friends treating them like family and enjoying fellowship sweet. Leonard and his beautiful wife Sophie had three small children who came to the preschool each morning carrying treats of fruit for us all to enjoy. Jeremiah led our praise and worship. This man of God shined with the joy of the Lord every time we saw him. His wife Jane would make the most amazing banana bread and gave each family a food parcel on Monday evening with that fresh aroma wafting in the air. Alan also met a brother called Jared on his first visit. Alan joined a team ministering in the local town. Alan and Jared also worked together on Mercy Ministry where God blessed their friendship which grew deep and strong. His family helped us to really appreciate the African way of life. I can remember one weekend they came to stay at our tiny home. The two families went into town and while walking down the street I needed to use the restroom. Being new to the area I asked directions to the bathroom. He took my hand and we ran across the street to a "box" standing alone. "In there," he said and opened the door. To my amazement someone had stolen the toilet, there was just a hole in the ground. I came out and told him and he laughed until tears streamed down his face. On seeing this, his wife came over and took me to a REAL bathroom. How grateful I was!

The first six months we were full-time Bible students of a discipleship training school and after graduation became full-time volunteer staff. All staff members spoke English when we were together however we did try to learn Swahili in order to reach the town people with the gospel of Jesus Christ. Alan worked with Mercy Ministry and took food and clothing to the leper colony. Leprosy is a mildly contagious disease that damages skin, internal organs and bones. It deadens sensation of the nerves. People with leprosy cannot feel pebbles that are stuck in their sandals, so they get open sores on their feet. They can't determine what pressure to use when turning a key or moving a log and so they may tear their skin. Leprosy leads to gangrene, paralysis and deformity.

On one of these occasions he walked down the stone stairway that had been cut into the rock and out into the enclosure that held many sick people. Through an interpreter Alan asked for them to "come out." Very slowly and one by one the men came out shouting for him to go away. But Alan stood by faith in the Son of God who loved him and gave Himself for him. That's my man! Lives were touched by the power of God that very day and Alan was a welcome guest forever.

My work was in the preschool, learning as I taught. How smart is God! As you already know from previous chapters I struggled at school missing a lot of the basic requirements needed to build a strong educational foundation. (Phew! Long words!) God had me read it, learn it, teach it and together we built it. Jeremiah 29 verse 11 makes it clear that God knows what He is doing when we read, *"For I know the plans I have for you declares the Lord. Plans to prosper you and not harm you, plans to give you hope and a future."NIV* These are the words from the Bible, words of encouragement from God Himself.

It was on one of these days while walking to the preschool that I saw our son Richie climbing up a sticky tree that was right next to a ship container. Its heavy steel doors were wide open showing the tools inside that were used for maintenance. As I passed by my son I called to him to be very careful, that tree is very slippery, and headed into the preschool to set things up for the children. A few minutes went by then I heard a piercing scream that froze my heart. The school door burst open and I was told my son had fallen. Not only had he fallen but in doing so caught his left arm on the open steel door slicing through almost everything. Only a piece of skin held the now dangling lifeless limb. Richie was conscious and fully aware of his situation. Blood covered his shirt and shorts. Everyone sprang into action. Transport was found and he was loaded in. Alan and I with the driver and one staff member raced to the ferry only to find it on the other side of the Indian Ocean unloading. God meets us in the midst of fear and doubt, giving his frightened child comfort and peace that He is in control. In prayer we asked God to make a way for the ferry to come as fast as possible. An emergency signal went out and within minutes the ferry came over empty and took only our car to the other side. We raced to Mombasa hospital all the while watching our son slowly lose sight of his surroundings.

The doctor packed his arm with ice and told us to take a seat. A little later Richie was wheeled into the operating room where he remained for several hours. During this time Alan and I were on our knees before the Lord seeking God's favor in this situation. Even in the depth of despair the Lord is with us (Ps. 139:8 NIV). The door opened and out came the surgeon looking puzzled saying, "I have seen the extent of this injury and taken tests for much needed blood but I have to tell you both I just don't understand it." Shaking his head, he went on to say to us, "Your son has NOT lost the blood normal to this type of injury. No blood donation is needed for this operation." We looked at him and cried. He said as he looked at us on our knees, "Keep doing whatever it is you are doing because IT WORKS!" and then he was gone. We were so encouraged by this and began thanking and praising the Lord. God was doing a miracle right before our eyes. Close to eight hours later we were allowed to see our son.

I stayed with Richie for the 19 days he was in the hospital and during that time, Rebecca and Matthew were admitted with malaria and Alan soon followed them. Dee was home alone. I knew that good friends were keeping her safe and making sure she went to school each day. Dee was the backbone that kept our family together with her positive and happy attitude lifting our spirits toward the throne of grace. Alan and the children were released from hospital after a few days of treatment and I thank God they never came back sick again.

On day ten of Richie's stay in the hospital the doctors told him he would have to go to the hospital in Nairobi for treatment they could not offer. Nairobi was three hundred miles away. Richie looked at me, then at the doctor and said, "If God wants to heal my arm He can do it right here. I don't have to go anywhere."

The doctor left looking sad. For Richie, it was his faith in God that moved the heart of God to begin a miracle that would remind us all of God's unconditional love.

I could understand the doctor's concern because my son's arm was turning black, indicating a lack of blood supply at the injured site. The day after Richie made his confession of faith in God we noticed the tips of his fingers turning pink. Over the next couple of days his entire arm returned to its normal color. Day 18 came and as the African nurse was gently cleaning around the two silver pins that held the pieces of arm together, one of the pins ejected itself from my son's arm and slid across the hospital floor. She burst into Swahili and ran to the phone to call the doctor who came within minutes. He took over the cleaning, making sure to stay away from the remaining pin when out it flew and hit the floor with a beautiful "ting!" I'm sorry, but we couldn't contain ourselves. Richie and I wet our pants laughing, and crying happy tears. We were ever thankful to our mighty faithful Father that our son's healing was in God's hands all the time.

The following year it was my turn to be a guest of Mombasa hospital; not once but twice. I had been admitted due to severe weight loss. Some of my hair had fallen out and I lost 24 pounds in two months. Doctors could not find the cause, so I was sent home still very weak and unable to walk on my own.

The devil was playing with my mind. One day a brother in the Lord came to pray with me. I asked him if I was going to die. He was quiet for a few minutes, then he took my hand in his and said kindly, "This sickness will not end in death." His words gave me the hope I needed to believe for my total healing. A few days later I was back in the hospital unable to move. They ran more tests— all came back negative.

I lay there asking God what was going on with my body. I closed my eyes to shut out the activity of the ward when I felt someone sitting on my bed. I opened my eyes to see a young man in a white coat sitting looking at me. "You are to get up and go home," he said. I didn't know this man so I told him I was unable to move. He reached forward and gently laid his hand on my arm just above my right hand. Shock waves traveled up my arm and filled every part of my being with such an energy force I'm sure I could have climbed a mountain. I reached forward to turn his ID badge around so I could address him by name when he disappeared right before my eyes. I threw back the blankets, walked down two flights of stairs and called the mission to come and get me. Shortly after my family and I went home to England!

God's grace was revealed in Mombasa in the many victories that were won over the powers of darkness.

> *Romans 8:31-32*, "What then shall we say in response to this? If God is for us who can be against us? He (God) who did not spare His own Son but gave Him up for us all, how will He also along with Him graciously give us all things."

COME WALK WITH ME

Chapter Seven
OPEN DOORS

Returning to cold wet England after spending two glorious years in the heat of Mombasa took some getting used to. As a family we had no idea what the future held but we were not concerned for we knew who held our future.

We were well and strong again within a few months. Our home church stood with us in prayer seeking what God would have us do next. We were blessed by the kindness of others and given a small house to live in for the months that followed.

During that time, a wedding invitation arrived from a lady I had become close friends with in Kenya. Lori had been my prayer partner and closest friend during our time in Kenya. She had such a beautiful spirit and a smile to match. She arrived at the mission base knowing no one so the leadership sent her to our little home. That was the beginning of an amazing friendship that I will treasure forever. Lori had returned to Minnesota to get married and asked if I would come to the States and be her matron of honor in the wedding. My husband Alan applied for a visa to visit the USA and we waited for this to arrive.

One day Alan and I went to town and I phoned Lori from a pay phone to let her know that Alan had sent off the request for a USA visa. We talked with great excitement about seeing each other again, about the upcoming wedding, about all sorts of things that girls talk about and never seem to run out of things to say. I hung up the receiver and stood very still. I heard another voice, a voice that got my full attention, a voice that had something I needed to hear. God spoke clearly to my heart while I stood inside the phone booth. "If you are willing to give this up, I will give you something better." He only said it once. It was my choice and not a demand from God.

I came out of the phone booth to my waiting husband and shared with him what God had said to me. Alan's loving arms went around me and he drew me into his embrace not saying a word. I could feel the tears welling up in my eyes. I so wanted to be with my dearest, sweetest friend on her special day, but I also wanted to please God. That Saturday evening Alan and I committed the wedding invite and the "something better" to the Lord. Sunday morning while leaving church we asked a brother who lived some twenty miles away from us to seek the Lord on our behalf about the trip to the United States for the wedding. Barry had been a close and trusted friend that shone with the love of Christ. He spoke of the tenderness of the Savior and forgiveness that comes through true repentance. Barry said he would spend the afternoon alone and wait on the Lord. Should the Lord give him scripture for us then he would call and let us know. After lunch the children took their naps as I went upstairs alone to seek the Lord. Alan was downstairs alone with his Bible and note pad. Barry called later in the afternoon saying he had heard from the Lord on our behalf and was coming over to share with us. He sounded so excited! When Barry arrived Alan and I met him in the kitchen with what God had given to each one of us. Sitting around the kitchen table the three of us opened up the scripture we had been given.

Proverbs 25:25 *"Like cold water to a weary soul is good news from a distant land."*

Each one of us had the same scripture! The next day in the morning mail the visa to the USA arrived. Little did we know what God had done on our behalf but it was soon going to be made abundantly clear. That my friend is how God works.

Through the leading of the Holy Spirit we applied to return to the mission field overseas. The first mission base that replied was a place called Saipan. We checked this out and found that Saipan is one of fourteen islands in the Commonwealth Marianas Islands. The island is seven miles wide and fourteen miles long; a beautiful tropical island in the western Pacific Ocean. "Hafa Ada," is the greeting from the friendly Chamorro people. Alan and I believed God had opened the door for us to return to full time overseas mission work so Alan applied to the mission base there. They told him he would need to apply for a special kind of visa to be allowed to come to the CNMI (Commonwealth of the Northern Marianas Islands). This visa, the B1 B2 visa, was extremely hard to get, but it was the only way we could enter Saipan. We had not looked over the visa carefully that had come a few days before so Alan took it out of the drawer, opened it up and there stamped in bright red letters was B1 B2 visa. We hugged and danced and cried all at the same time. Yes, God had given us something better because we gave up what we wanted. Yes, God had gone before us knowing our hearts are to please Him and Him alone.

We made August of 1989 to be our departure date from England to Saipan. Little did we know that not all of our children would be going with us. Dee came to ask us if she could stay in England and go to college there. I was not prepared emotionally for saying yes to this request. Dee told me that she had met a family that was willing to let her stay with them while we were overseas. Roy and Maureen loved Dee from day one and she them. Alan and I felt good about this arrangement as the Lord stilled our hearts with confirmation it was the right thing to do.

Guam is 7,454 miles from England and our first place to stay for a few weeks before making the final flight of 215 km to Saipan. I remember getting off the plane at Saipan International Airport and my clothes stuck to me with the heat of the day. I just smiled. It was beautiful, a paradise to behold. It would be our home for as long as God wants us to stay. The welcome at the airport by the island people with music and flowers made this first day a memory we will cherish forever. On the island of Saipan was a missionary gospel organization called Far Eastern Broadcasting Company or F.E.B.C. They had an open house to welcome all the new missionaries to the island. Alan and I took the children and it was at this event that the next step in God's plan was about to unfold. We were introduced to a man, Jim, and his four children. Soon all the kids were off playing somewhere. Jim, Alan, and I talked most of the afternoon and before we left we invited him and his family to the mission base the next free day they had. Jim brought his beautiful, very shy wife, Naomi, to our house the very next day. The guys were outside watching the kids play while Naomi and I sat inside my house: me talking, her listening. She did say two words to me that first day, "hello" and "good-bye!" I liked her right away. This was going to be my new best friend. I knew deep in my heart that God would make a way for this friendship to blossom and grow over time. I missed Dee so very much and longed to have a girl to hang out with.

Jim and Naomi had arrived on the island earlier that year and had taken the opportunity to explore with their four children the wonders of God's beautiful creation. Jim liked to scuba dive and found a cave called the Grotto that was perfect for this hobby. Jim, Alan and our two sons were certified divers. This made the buddy system of diving perfect. Most weekends as Jim's schedule allowed, the guys would make a date to dive and Naomi and I would hang out at her house watching movies with the younger children in the air conditioned room.

From August to December I taught in the local Christian school where more than five hundred children were in attendance. From January on I established a free preschool for any child wanting to learn. The first year I had two children, Jennifer and Wilson. The second year I had two full classes of children from many different nationalities: Chamorro, Korean, Japanese and American, all happy to be learning together. God had clearly told me to offer this ministry completely free to any child and in obedience to Him that is what I did. God added his blessing to this work. In the summer of the third year I put together a portfolio of my vision for the preschool and its needs and made myself known to every business on the island. Funds came in to start the work of building a new school. That same year Jim and Naomi told us they were going back to the States for good. It was emotionally difficult for us all, as our friendship had grown deep roots of love and respect.

We promised to try and keep in touch as best we could. Cell phones had not yet been invented: no Face book, no Face time. Snail mail was the only way to keep the connection flowing, and sometimes it seemed the snail had no intention of moving at all!

God started working in the hearts of the island people once they knew our desire to serve them. Alan and I moved to another part of the island and established Stepping Stones Ministries. This ministry would give us the flexibility to incorporate outreach into the local prison and into the homes of the local people and win the trust and respect of all. In 1992 Stepping Stones Ministries started a free preschool. This school ran two full classes ten months a year. I had the full support of every parent whose child was enrolled. We were treated just like family. I smile as I remember one incident when I was teaching the children in the front part of our home. Many of the fathers had come early to pick up their children. While waiting, they sat around my kitchen table and decided that the English food I had made for the Bible study that night looked yummy so they helped themselves to it until all fifty pastries were gone. What an honor that was to me! Food and family go hand in hand on Saipan Island.

One of the ways we returned the kindness to the many companies that helped us get re-established as a ministry was to visit each one during the month of December and present the story of the birth of Christ which the children acted out. Twenty-four children, and about the same amount of parents visited twelve companies for our outreach program. God did a mighty work through the children's ministry. We saw lives touched and changed by the power of the Holy Spirit. Each year two families would adopt one company to bless with a small gift and a school photograph thanking them for their kindness to us. Stepping Stones had a love feast close to Christmas where we invited every sponsor to join us at the school (which was our home) for this special time. One by one the sponsors would be called up to the front and two children would give them their gift of thanks. I can honestly say that the preschool lacked for nothing because we serve a God who is more than enough.

Anytime there was a party everyone would help. Food preparation started three days before the party because it was the local custom for each person to take a plate of food home to enjoy the next day. I remember my first fiesta. Six-foot long tables touching end to end filled the center of the yard and were laden down with very large containers filled with all kinds of food, full to over flowing. As I reached the end of the line with my plate of food piled high, the host was waiting with tin foil, took my plate from me and wrapped it before giving it back with the instructions of filling a clean plate for that night's dinner. It would have been an insult to them not to do as requested.

My husband joined a prison ministry team already going into the local prison and it was not long before Alan inherited this ministry. Alan held Bible studies there once a week. It was during this time I helped train the inmates for their Christmas outreach program to their families. The preschool was asked to present their Christmas program to the inmates at the local prison. Once we arrived in full costume of Mary, Joseph, three wise men, an angel, shepherds and manger, it was discovered that the manger would not fit through the main doors into the prison. The only way was to lift the manger up over the outer prison walls and lower it down on the other side. The children and I stood in awe as our Bible study brothers made this happen and the play was a blessing to all.

Word got around the island of the work of Stepping Stones Ministries. Alan felt God's favor as he went from company to company asking for donations of toys for the inmates' families. These were gift wrapped and tagged before the Christmas inmates program. How God moved! How God blessed! These dear inmates learned five animated Bible songs and between each song a brother would share his testimony of the transformation of his life under the power of a mighty God. One song spoke about God's forgiveness.

Romans 8:1 NIV, "There is therefore now no condemnation to those who are in Christ Jesus."

These dear brothers in the Lord gave a Holy Spirit inspired performance of a new life touched and transformed by the power of a loving and compassionate God. After the performance the inmates gave out the gifts to their family members. Each child and every wife received a gift from their loved one. I cried with joy seeing the families reunited within the walls of family love.

During our time on Saipan, Richie met and fell in love with a beautiful American lady— Amy. They married and not long afterwards moved to the States with their son Mason.

Chapter Eight
GOD'S VISION REVEALED

Jim did come to visit us and a year or so later Naomi came. It was so good to see them both and catch up on family and ministry news. Alan was happy to have Jim staying with us and the two spent many happy hours doing guy stuff. I can still see Jim taking all twenty-four students out into the school yard, making a big circle and teaching them to work every muscle by following him in the art of keep fit. I stood behind the stone pillar and smiled with delight. How this blessed my soul! Then it was time for Naomi to visit. The students liked her right away. She took my morning Bible hour and had the students in fits of laughter as she told stories with grunts and groans of how David defeated Goliath (1 Samuel chapter 17). She told them it doesn't matter how big the problem is or how big the person is; God is bigger! David won because of his faith in God. God is on the side of faith. The children asked if she could teach Bible hour every school day so she did until the school holidays started the end of that week. Now Naomi and I had time to see the island together.

One of the preschool parents had given us a free all-inclusive first-class weekend on the island of Tinian, a ferry ride away. The Dynasty Hotel where we stayed was magnificent in every way. Tinian is well known for its hot peppers but also for its launching of the atomic bomb attack against Hiroshima and Nagasaki, Japan.

The day after we arrived on the Island of Tinian we went for a walk. On the way back to the hotel, Naomi hurt her foot on a sharp coral. Me being a bright spark took out of my bag a five-dollar bill and wrapped this around her big toe to stop the bleeding. We were some distance from our hotel and Naomi was having trouble walking— time for prayer. I turned around to see a car coming towards us. A kind gentleman took us to our hotel where her foot received the very best care possible.

Time came too soon for Naomi to return to the States. While saying our goodbyes at the Saipan International Airport we both tried to be brave and keep the conversation light yet our hugs said, "Will we ever see each other again this side of heaven?" Only God knew the answer to that question. It would be several years before He shared the answer with us.

After ten years of missionary service on the island of Saipan, and with a very successful ministry in full swing in the preschool, prison and community, Alan and I decided to return to England. Dee was over the moon to have her parents and siblings back home again. We made sure to do happy family things as much as possible. Dee excelled in college. She had grown into a very beautiful young woman. Often I would look at her when she was preoccupied and see David, her birth father, in her smile. Her tenderness towards her siblings was filled with laughter and fun. She was the big sister, reading bedtime stories and playing. Our family was once again complete after ten years of being apart.

A year later I went for a visit to Jim and Naomi and while at a Bible study, God spoke to my heart about our family moving to live in the USA. God had the plan. God had a purpose. God had the timing all worked out.

This time it was our daughter Rebecca who asked if she could stay in England and complete her college education. Emotions ran high in me. I had to be reassured by God that granting her request was the right thing to do. Alan and I went to prayer we placed a fleece before the Lord. If a family offered to care for her like a family did for Dee, then we would know this was the will of God for Rebecca. A family offered so we left England with only one of our four children to start this new adventure God had made possible for us.

In 2001 we moved to the States and a new and exciting chapter unfolded right before our eyes. Jim and Naomi, our dear friends on Saipan, invited us to move in with them until we could find a home of our own. Alan started working for a substance abuse treatment center in Lansing, Michigan. Alan and I had been seeking God about the house he wanted us to have. We decided to put out a fleece just like Gideon did when he wanted to know God's will (Judges 6:36-40). The following year God showed us the house he wanted to give us as our home.

What was Gideon's fleece? We read in Judges 6:36-37 these words…

Judges 6:36-37 ³⁶*Then Gideon said, 'If you will save Israel by my hand as you have said,* ³⁷ *behold I am laying a fleece of wool on the threshing floor. If there is dew on the fleece alone, and it is dry on all the ground, then I shall know that you will save Israel by my hand.'"*

We all want to be sure we are doing the will of God. We can ask God to give us signs along the pathway of life. I'm sure he does but do we see them as signs from God?

Alan and I put out our fleece to God about the right house to buy. The only person that knew our fleece was God. We looked at several houses for sale but none of them had the fleece. "What was our fleece?" I hear you asking. Alan and I told God this will be our sign: that the house He wants us to have will be sold with their family dog. Now how many people do you know sell their family pet with their home? We received a phone call from friends telling us the house next to theirs was up for sale and we should check it out so we did. The owners showed us the house. It had all of our requirements: three bedrooms, two bathrooms and land. While sitting at their kitchen table the lady told us we could only buy their house if we took their family dog, too. That's how we knew this house was the home God gave us as His gift to enjoy. The owners never understood the tears of gratitude rolling down my face because these tears were for answered prayers to a faithful God. The dog was a husky who looked just like a snow wolf. Her coat of white and grey was so very soft to touch. Her big blue eyes completed the beauty of this magnificent creature. She seemed to adjust well to her new English family.

In 2002 Naomi and I were asked to help at the local alternative school here in Nashville, Michigan. We were told that young mothers had dropped out of school and wanted to come back to complete their education. I knew first-hand what it is like not to have an education. After much prayer and talking it through, Naomi and I offered to work the one day a week that they asked for and the girls returned to school. Within a month we helped out five days a week and at one point had nineteen children under five between the two of us. That first year the school gave us a portable classroom to share with another group of students. It was a little crowded but we made it work for the sake of the young mothers. The second year we had a portable of our own and "Mothers' Helpers" was born.

It took us ten hours a day most of that summer, scrubbing and painting, to get the portable ready for the new school year. Long before anyone arrived, Naomi and I would seek the Lord on behalf of our daycare parents, children and ministry. The doors opened at 7:45 A.M. and children of all sizes and conditions were handed over to us. The mornings were very busy with hands-on activities, snack time as well as diapering and feeding the babies. The mothers came at lunchtime, which gave us thirty minutes to set up the afternoon program. At 11:45 A.M. the children were back, ready for naptime. Some days it took us an hour or so before the precious little ones were washed, diapered and ready to nap. Naomi and I would read Bible stories to them before they went to sleep and sing while stroking or rocking them. Dim lights helped the little ones to relax. Two senior ladies helped out once a week rocking our newborns. The mothers would pick up their children around three in the afternoon and ask how the day went for their child. Their artwork of the day made many parents smile with delight. Once the charts and cleaning were done off home we would go some days as late as six only to do it all again the next day.

Naomi and I saw this as our ministry because very often the parents would sit and talk with us well into the evening. It took time for them to trust us and feel comfortable in sharing their lives with us; however, genuine love won the day, as the daycare became one big family. During the third year Naomi and I decided we would like to do something special to be a blessing to our daycare parents so we talked to Jennifer at Barry Community Foundation. She listened with great excitement and before long came on board and blessed us with toys and a check for clothing for our families. Taking all our moms shopping at once was truly an adventure! They were each given an amount to buy appropriate school clothing for themselves and their children. We had one dad in our program at that time, Chip. He came into the daycare one day to play with his child, so we asked him to remove his shoes before stepping on our white carpet. Chip looked embarrassed as he slowly removed his shoes. We saw that both mismatched socks were full of holes. Time to take this young dad shopping! I never realized how long that would take. He looked at every t-shirt available to him, every pair of long pants, every hoodie, every pair of sneakers. We were in this one store for hours! Chip had chosen well. Upon going to pay for his items he asked Naomi and I if he had any money left over to get a watch. She told him to go and find the one he wanted and as he walked away she turned at me and smiled. No words were needed. We knew God would cover the cost of Chip's watch no matter how much it came to. The next day Chip came into the daycare wearing his new clothes. "Ta da!" he said with hands stretched out and wearing the biggest smile on his beautiful face we had ever seen.

At graduation we made caps and gowns for the daycare children so they could walk with their parents across the stage and receive their preschool diploma. By the time the government closed our school down we had served seven years and every one of our parents graduated. Such a privilege! Such an honor!

COME WALK WITH ME

Chapter Nine
MISSION ESTABLISHED

Over the next few months, families from the daycare and the community called us to ask if we had daycare available for them. I felt in my heart this would be a good way to continue serving families in our community. Naomi and I prayed and talked over the possibility of having the daycare set up in her home. With the license and inspection completed we continued serving families in need. God brought many hours of happiness with these beautiful children. Our friendship with the families grew and blossomed.

I remember one summer we decided to have a

family fun day. One of the parents offered the use of their lawn. Naomi and I went shopping for the things we would need for the games. Being the creative type, I decided to make a fancy dress race. I went to our local thrift shop and collected items of ladies' clothing far too big to fit anyone. This was going to be fun! I arranged the fathers in a line. When the music started the fathers would run as fast as possible, pick up and put on the first piece of clothing then run to the next and so on until they reached the finished line fully outfitted. The watching families rolled in fits of laughter seeing their dad make this game into a happy memory to cherish forever. It wasn't about the winner or the prize it was all about family fun. We laughed until our sides hurt!

Family fun is God's highest for his children. Families are important to God. Being a part of the family of God is the greatest blessing given to the believer and should drive us to our knees in appreciation for who God is. The invitation to be part of God's family is universal but there is one condition: faith in Jesus.

Galatians 3:26 NIV "You are all children through faith in Christ Jesus."

There are only two ways to get into a family. You can either be born into it or you can be adopted into it. God does both for us. It's called being born again. God says we are not only born again into His family, but He has adopted us and there is no way that He will ever give us up. We belong to the family of God. Christ accepted us so we can accept each other.

Romans 15:6-7 NIV "So that with one heart and mouth you may glorify the God and Father of our Lord Jesus Christ. Accept one another then, just as Christ accepted you."

Believers are brothers and sisters in Christ no matter where they live.

I remember how I met a young woman named Sherri. She came from the Lansing area, about an hour drive from my house. This sweet tenderhearted lady was going to give me a run for my money. In other words, she would help move me out of my comfort zone so that God could and would show to me His constant protection. I smile as I remember back to how we met. I was going with Alan to a very small church near our home. This was one of the Sundays I was not working. The pastor asked if someone could drive for Sherri for one year. She had lost her driver's license due to health issues and wanted to continue fellowshipping with other believers she already knew. I sat there waiting for someone to step up but no one did. At the end of the service the pastor asked again, and again I waited expecting one of her friends to answer. I didn't even own a car of my own so how could I help? The next thing I knew I was on my feet answering Sherri's need. Little did I know this was all part of God's plan.

I have never been good at remembering directions when it comes to driving in any location I have not visited at least one hundred times before. God wanted me to grow. God wanted me to trust Him. God wanted me to know that He would never leave me or forsake me— no matter what. He provided a car, Sherri gave me her car to use for the year at no personal expense. Driving for Sherri was a blessing in disguise and only time would make that blessing abundantly clear.

In order to stay true to my commitment to drive for Sherri every Sunday, I would have to get up extra early and go to bed later than normal, no big deal. I would have to drive through Michigan winters on the freeway— oh no! Snow and icy roads— now it was a big deal! It's easy to let fear replace faith, I know because I did just that. You see, what I failed to remember was God had this fully under His control. I had to learn to look at the Savior and not the situation. In other words, I had to focus my mind on His ability and not my own; on His knowledge and not my lack of understanding. Only thirty miles eight times a day once a week was not much to ask of Him to watch over me, and He did far more than watch over me, He gave me the gift of this sweet lady who soon became a dear friend. I would drive the thirty miles to pick her up each Sunday and she would tell me all about her week on the drive back to Nashville for church. Once the morning service was over I would drive her home and we would talk about the morning's sermon and how we could apply it to our life. Three hours later we were doing it all again. One weekend a month I would be invited to stay in her guest room and on these occasions we would talk about the Lord well into the night.

Sherri was so hungry for the Word of God to fill her to overflowing. She would sit and listen to me going on and on and… well, you get the picture I'm sure. Sherri's heart was to serve the Lord without question. Sherri had a natural way to make people feel loved. On Mother's Day she brought a long stem red roses for every mother in our church. Even though she was not a mother herself she displayed a mother's heart in all she did for others.

When the year was up and Sherri began to driver herself again she stayed with Alan and me between church services. She had become a very good cook and surprised us with amazing dishes to enjoy. We would play games or take a nap before the evening service. Our friendship had grown over time from friends to sisters.

She would often write to me. One letter she wrote said, "I put up walls over the years to keep from being hurt again. But you, Miss Elly (as she called me) were like a bull in a china store and broke them all down. I find peace flooding my soul as I listen to you talk about the Lord. I watch as your face becomes a beacon of light shining forth your deep love and devotion for the Savior of your heart. Our friendship means more to me than words can express. I find myself wanting to call you but refrain because I just did call you. There is not much that I wouldn't do for you, Miss Elly, and in the years to come I will show you how much I appreciate you as my dearest friend and sister in the Lord."

Philippians 1:6 *"Being confident of this very thing, that he who began a good work in you will perfect it until the day of Jesus Christ."*

Sherri was confident that God was perfecting His perfect will in and through her. She loved Him. She worshipped Him. She lived for her Savior. His light and love shined through her life to all.

One weekend the police stopped her for

speeding on her way to see me. When she told me this was the only ticket she had ever had for speeding I couldn't help but laugh. Sherri was laughing too when she handed me her car keys and said, "My car is now yours!" Sam gave me a 2005 Michigan blue Chevy Cobalt which I still drive to this day. I went with her to get her new car that was ready for pick up. It was blue, too. I asked her why she was not keeping the Chevy and she said with a smile, "No cruise control."

She had such a great sense of humor. She often had me in tears with laughter. Being friends with Sherri reminds me of Philippians 1:6.

Philippians 1:6 NIV "Being confident of this very thing, that he who began a good work in you will perfect it until the day of Jesus Christ."

By her life Sherri showed me her confidence that God was perfecting His perfect will in and through her. She inspired me in her love of God and in her exuberant worship of Him. She lived for her Savior and to show His light and love through her life to all.

How rich my life has become! All these blessings given to me by Almighty God! As I look back over my Christian walk I am forever grateful for each and every one of them that God has brought into my life. Yes, I am rich; rich in kingdom values, rich in precious friends, rich in unconditional agape love, rich having given my heart over to the safe keeping of a loving God. I am forever thankful that my walk with Jesus Christ leading the way will be a walk of faith in the Son of God who loved me and gave Himself for me.

"He lives! He lives!
Christ Jesus lives today.
He walks with me and talks with me
Along life's narrow way.
He lives! He lives!
Salvation to impart.
You ask me how I know He lives?
He lives within my heart."

My Savior lives and one day we will share eternity together.

COME WALK WITH ME

Chapter Ten
FROM RECKLESS TO REDEEMED

How do I say thank you to all the wonderful people that have shared my life? My life is richly blessed because of each one of them and their personal sacrifice made on my behalf.

My five children: Cordelia, Devlin, Richard,
                     Rebecca and Matthew.

Dee   My beautiful first born daughter, for
         staying strong and carrying on.
Devlin   Safe in the loving arms of Jesus

Richard	For displaying your shield of faith.
Rebecca	Believing the best in everyone
Matthew	Giving hope to others

My wonderful partners in life:

David	For loving me regardless
Alan	Holding me with tenderness

Dear Friends:

Graham	For leading me to the Lord— my first spiritual father
Heather	Spiritual mother & mentor
Hillary	Teaching me to read
Andy	For letting her
Carol	Being a blessing
Laurie	Taking care of my children
Naomi	Unconditional love
Jim	Gracious kindness
Pastor	Teaching me God's highest priorities
Sherri	Your contagious sense of humor
Debbie	Editing this project to completion

Reckless to Redeemed - that's me. I will live, and serve, and worship until Jesus takes me home.

I will always be grateful that God saw me worthy to be His kingdom child forever. I remember the words of a wounded mother of long ago that told me, "You are worthless." Not so, in God's eyes I am priceless. Words that told me, "You will never amount to anything." Not so, I amounted to the greatest and highest level possible - that of a precious child of God. I know who I am in the family of God. I know my worth. I know my value. I know that I am unconditionally loved by my heavenly Father, love not tainted by this world but pure as gold.

In March of 2016 I was ordained by my local church here in Michigan into the five-fold ministry as mentioned in Ephesians 4 verse 11. This verse describes apostles, prophets, evangelists, pastors or shepherds and teachers staying active in the body of Christ. Pastor David has taken time to mentor me in kingdom values. This mighty man of God became my second spiritual father after Graham who led me to the Lord so long ago in my kitchen in England. Papa, as I call him, filled my life with exciting adventures from the word of God. He challenged me to *"seek first the kingdom of God and His righteousness and all these things shall be added unto you." **Matthew 6:33-34 NIV**. Papa would always teach that my life must line up with the word of God. In other words, ask what would Jesus do in any given situation then do likewise. I believe God led me to my present church under the teachings of Pastor David so that I may experience the fullness of God's unending love, mercy and grace.

<u>GRACE</u>

G God's
R righteousness
A at
C Christ's
E expense

Author's Note

Come Walk with Me has really been a work of God. The Spirit of the Lord worked in me and through me to make it abundantly clear that to God I have value; to God I am loved; to God I am forgiven.

To walk with God is to know His peace, love and mercy at every turn in the road of life. Jesus invited me to "walk with Him". I have never once regretted saying yes. Although I have given Him many reasons not to choose me, not to want me, not to forgive me, not to love me – none of these reasons changed His mind. I am loved of the Lord. "Come walk with Me," said Jesus, and I did just that.

The story doesn't end here. Book two of this trilogy, Come Lean on Me, will move you closer and deeper in love with the Savior of your soul. Supported by His ever loving arms, through all kinds of trials and tragedy there is inner peace of mind, body, soul and spirit. When death came knocking on my door not once or twice but three times, it was then I felt the strength of His embrace and the power of His love. His embrace that says, "I'm here for you."

I encourage you to continue with my story in Come Lean on Me. I know Jesus will meet you in your darkest hour to bring you into His marvelous light.